W9-CKI-762

AMAZON.COM

ABDO
Publishing Company

TECHNOLOGY PIONEERS

AMAZON.COM

THE COMPANY AND ITS FOUNDER

by Erika Wittekind

Content Consultant
Robert Spector
Founder & Chairman,
Robert Spector Consulting

CREDITS

Printed in the United States of America,
North Mankato, Minnesota
052012
092012

 THIS BOOK CONTAINS AT LEAST 10% RECYCLED MATERIALS.

Editor: Megan Anderson
Series Designer: Emily Love

Library of Congress Cataloging-in-Publication Data

Wittekind, Erika, 1980-
Amazon.com : the company and its founder / Erika Wittekind.
pages cm. -- (Technology pioneers)
Includes bibliographical references.
ISBN 978-1-61783-330-4
1. Amazon.com (Firm)--History--Juvenile literature. 2. Internet bookstores--United States--Juvenile literature. 3. Electronic commerce--United States--Juvenile literature. 4. Bezos, Jeffrey--Juvenile literature. 5. Booksellers and bookselling--United States--Biography--Juvenile literature. 6. Businessmen--United States--Biography--Juvenile literature. I. Title.
Z473.A485W58 2013
381'.4500202854678--dc23

2012005977

TABLE OF CONTENTS

CHAPTER 1

Amazon.com founder and CEO Jeff Bezos introduced the Kindle on November 19, 2007.

A NEW WAY TO READ

"This is the most important thing we've ever done," Amazon.com founder and Chief Executive Officer (CEO) Jeff Bezos told *Newsweek* in November 2007. "It's so ambitious to take something as highly evolved as the book and improve on it. And maybe even change the way people read."[1]

Amazon.com had just launched the Kindle, the company's first electronic reading device, also known as an e-reader. With this new product, the company was building on how it started in the 1990s—it was revolutionizing the way people purchased books. But this time, Amazon.com was also attempting to change the way people read them.

THE IDEA

Bezos was no stranger to introducing the world to a new way of doing something everyone took for granted. In 1995, he started Amazon.com as an online bookstore. Instead of walking into a bookstore, a consumer could conduct a simple search, place an order, and have books delivered to his or her door within days. The first successful e-commerce site, Amazon.com has since expanded to offer many other products and grown into an online global superstore.

Unlike the introduction of e-commerce, e-readers were not a new idea. Several devices were introduced in the 1990s. These devices failed to catch on due to their bulky size, eyestrain caused by reading backlit liquid crystal display (LCD) screens, and the limited selection of e-books available at the time.

But when Apple opened its iTunes store in 2003, Bezos took notice. The music store allowed users to instantly purchase and download music to their computers, iPods, and other MP3 players. Bezos thought that same instant access was possible for books—with the right device and a large enough inventory of e-books.

A fan of technology, Bezos also disliked the bulkiness of paper books. "I'm grumpy when I'm forced to read a physical book because it's not as convenient," he said. "Turning the pages . . . the book is always flopping itself shut at the wrong moment."[2] Bezos thought there must be a way to develop a successful e-reader and that Amazon.com was the one to do it.

PROJECT GUTENBERG

In 1971, Michael Hart, a student at the University of Illinois, Champaign-Urbana, started the first digital library, Project Gutenberg. The organization digitizes and archives public domain works. Public domain works are available for public use since they do not fall under copyright protection. The project started with Hart entering the Declaration of Independence into the school's computer system. He later transcribed other works, including the Bible. The world's oldest digital library, Project Gutenberg became a nonprofit organization in 2000 and has volunteers all over the world. Project Gutenberg had approximately 38,000 books in its archive as of February 2012.

In 2004, Amazon.com approached renowned hardware developer Gregg Zehr at Lab126 in Silicon Valley to begin developing the Kindle. Zehr, who had worked for Apple and palmOne, recruited other developers and went to work on what was originally a mysterious project. The Web site for Lab126 stated that they were working on a "ground-breaking, highly integrated consumer product."[3]

THE PRODUCT

When it came to developing the Kindle, Bezos knew he not only had to make something that was unique but also better than what people were accustomed to. "You can't ever

ELECTRONIC PAPER AND INK

Xerox Corporation's Palo Alto Research Center, where a researcher envisioned the first e-reader, developed the technology for electronic paper and electronic ink in the 1970s. The Sony Reader was the first e-reader to use electronic ink when it was released in 2006. It uses electrically charged particles that are black on one side and white on the other. The particles are flipped over using electric charges to create the appearance of black text on the screen.

The specific technology used by the Kindle came from E Ink Corporation, which slightly altered what the Xerox researchers had done. The display is filled with white particles that have a positive charge and black particles that have a negative charge. Using layers of charged electrodes, white and black particles are pulled to the top of the screen to form the black letters and white background. The particles look more like ink on a page than the electrons in computer screens. Because it needs to use power for only a brief moment each time it forms a new page, the electronic paper and ink system also preserves battery life, too.

outbook the book, so you have to do things that you can't do with a book," he said. "We have to build something better than a physical book."[4] That meant an easy-to-use device that provided a convenient way to put books on it and offer a broad selection of reading material—a combination so far no one had been able to achieve.

One e-reader, the Sony Reader, was released in the United States in 2006 for $299. Slimmer than previous e-reading devices, its display was the first to use "electronic ink" and "electronic paper" technology. This technology makes e-books look and feel to the eyes like regular paper and ink. But the Sony Reader device had no wireless capabilities, meaning consumers had to connect to their computers through a USB cable to load e-books. Sony also offered a limited selection of 20,000 e-books through its online store, Connect.

When the Kindle debuted, it had a simple touch screen and included Whispernet, technology that wirelessly connects the device to a network to download books from Amazon.com within seconds. Readers have access to immediately download any of the 90,000 electronic titles available on Amazon.com.

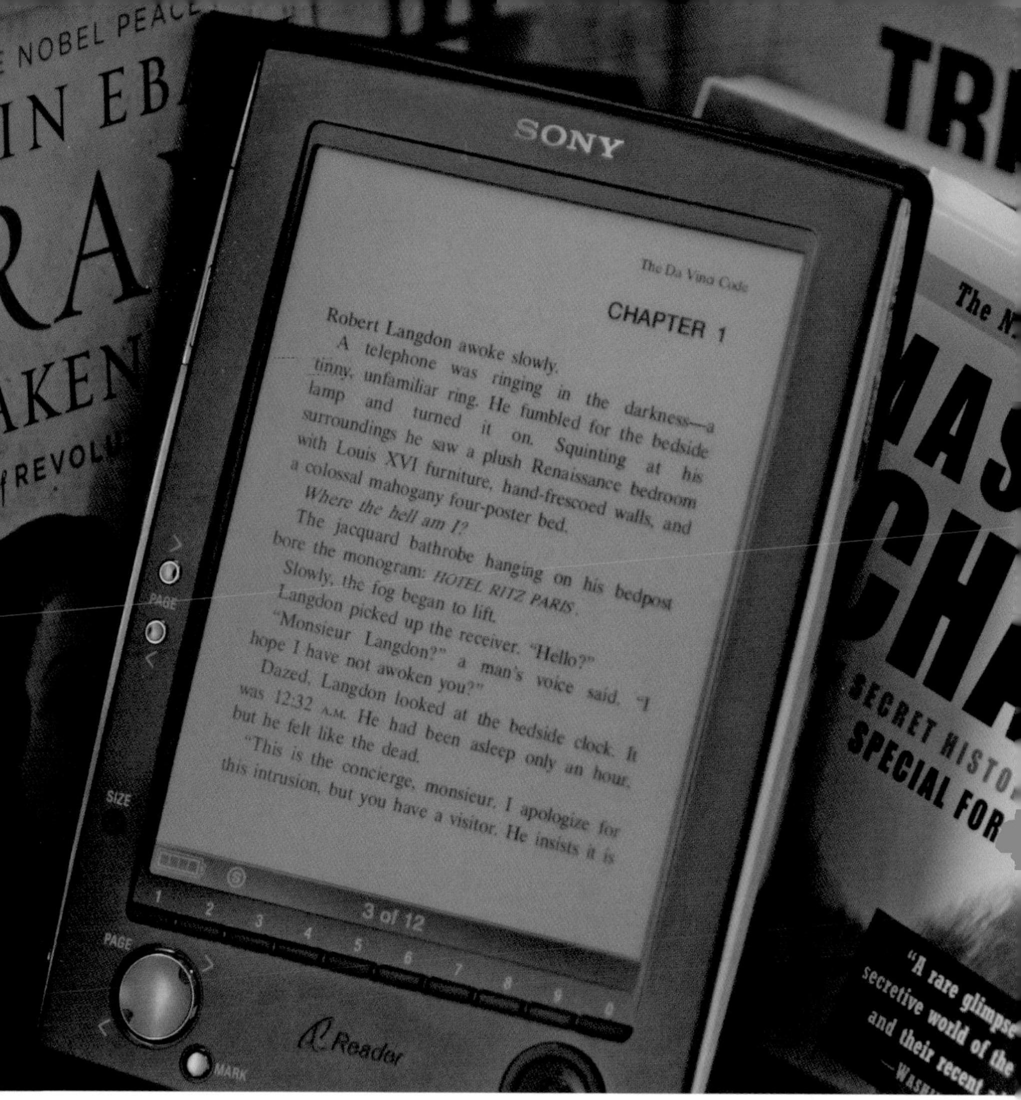

The Sony Reader in 2006

Giving the Kindle its wireless capability is what made the device stand out from other e-readers. In the book *Demand: Creating What People Love Before They Know They Want It* authors Karl Weber and Adrian Slywotzky wrote,

PRIMITIVE E-BOOKS

Beginning in 1993, Digital Book Inc. sold small sets of digitized books stored on floppy disks that could be accessed on a personal computer. The first e-book readers were Rocket eBook and SoftBook Reader, which were released in 1998 and sold for between $300 and $500. Approximately the size and thickness of a large book, these readers had LCD screens and could store as many as ten books at a time. Rocket eBook needed to be connected to a computer to download books; SoftBook Reader had a built-in modem. Everybook, introduced in 1999, was much more expensive at $1,600, but its twin screens attempted to simulate a real book. In 2000, the Gemstar company bought the makers of Rocket eBook and SoftBook Reader and launched the Gemstar eBook. In 2003, it was discontinued due to low sales.

. . . every added step, every extra restriction, every additional piece of gear needed to perform an activity makes a product dramatically less magnetic. Unplugging the PC wire gave Kindle users freedom—and gave the Kindle an essential touch of magic.[5]

Once an e-book is downloaded onto a Kindle, a user can simply highlight the book's title to open it. Each time the user opens a specific book, it automatically goes to the last page that was read. Not only does the Kindle have the convenience of almost-instant access to content, it has extra features. The reader can highlight a word and get a definition, change the font size, and search within the text. To reduce eyestrain, Lab126 developers incorporated the same electronic paper and electronic ink technology that was first available in the Sony Reader.

At 10.2 ounces (289.2 g), the original Kindle was lightweight and could store up to 200 e-books at once, meaning it was not only easier to carry around than printed books, but readers had access to a selection of books anywhere. Kindle users also had the option to pay a fee to subscribe and download newspapers, magazines, or blogs directly to their e-readers.

Compared to the Kindle, the Sony Reader offered less than a quarter of the selection of e-books offered through Amazon.com. Many people complained the Sony Reader had too many confusing buttons. Although it was not in the marketplace first, Bezos was banking on the Kindle being the first e-reader to surpass physical books in convenience and ease of use.

THE ROLLOUT

Still, skeptics expected consumers to balk at the price—$399 for the reader plus $10 per downloaded book. Others expected readers who had an attachment to the weight and feel of a paper book would continue to reject any electronic alternative.

FIRST FORAY INTO E-BOOKS

While developing the Kindle, Amazon.com rolled out a different way for customers to access books through its Web site. For several cents per page, customers could read parts of a book on their computer screens, or unlimited pages of a book for $1.99. Bezos knew customers would probably not want to read an entire book on a computer screen, but that the feature would be useful for someone who only wanted to read a shorter section of a book for reference or research purposes. Customers could also use the feature to sample books before buying a copy or to start reading before their copy arrived.

"Consumers have proven time and again that they would prefer to buy and keep physical books," analyst Evan Wilson told *Businessweek* in 2007.[6] Bezos rejected the notion that consumers would reject an e-reader in favor of physical books:

> *I've actually asked myself, "Why do I love these physical objects? Why do I love the smell of glue and ink?" The answer is that I associate that smell with all those worlds I have been transported to. What we love is the words and ideas.*[7]

Bezos appeared to be right; the first Kindles sold out within five and a half hours and were on back order for months. Amazon.com does not release sales figures for Kindles, but an estimated 240,000 units had sold by July 2008. Richard L. Brandt, author of *One Click: Jeff Bezos and the Rise of Amazon.com*, wrote about the immediate impact the introduction of the Kindle had on the publishing industry:

> *Since it was released, the question among publishers has gone from "Do people really want electronic books?" to "Do people want to read physical books anymore?" Jeff Bezos single-handedly turned publishing upside down with the Kindle.*[8]

The Kindle has continued to evolve since 2007. Amazon.com has released newer versions of the product, starting with the Kindle 2 in 2009. This version had a better display, improved battery life, and more storage than the original Kindle. Later in 2009, Amazon.com released the Kindle DX. It boasted a larger screen than the regular Kindle at 9.7 inches (24.6 cm).

E-reading has increased among consumers following the Kindle's release. In May 2010, Amazon.com announced that its e-book sales had begun to outpace sales for hardcover books. During the three previous months, Amazon.com had sold 143 e-books for every 100 hardcover books.

Amazon.com debuted its first color tablet, the Kindle Fire, in September 2011. In addition to reading books, the Kindle Fire allows users to watch movies, browse online, listen to music, and view other reading material such as magazines and newspapers.

Just as Bezos predicted, the Kindle changed the way people purchase books and other media. The technological shift continues to have wide-ranging effects on e-commerce and the publishing industry.

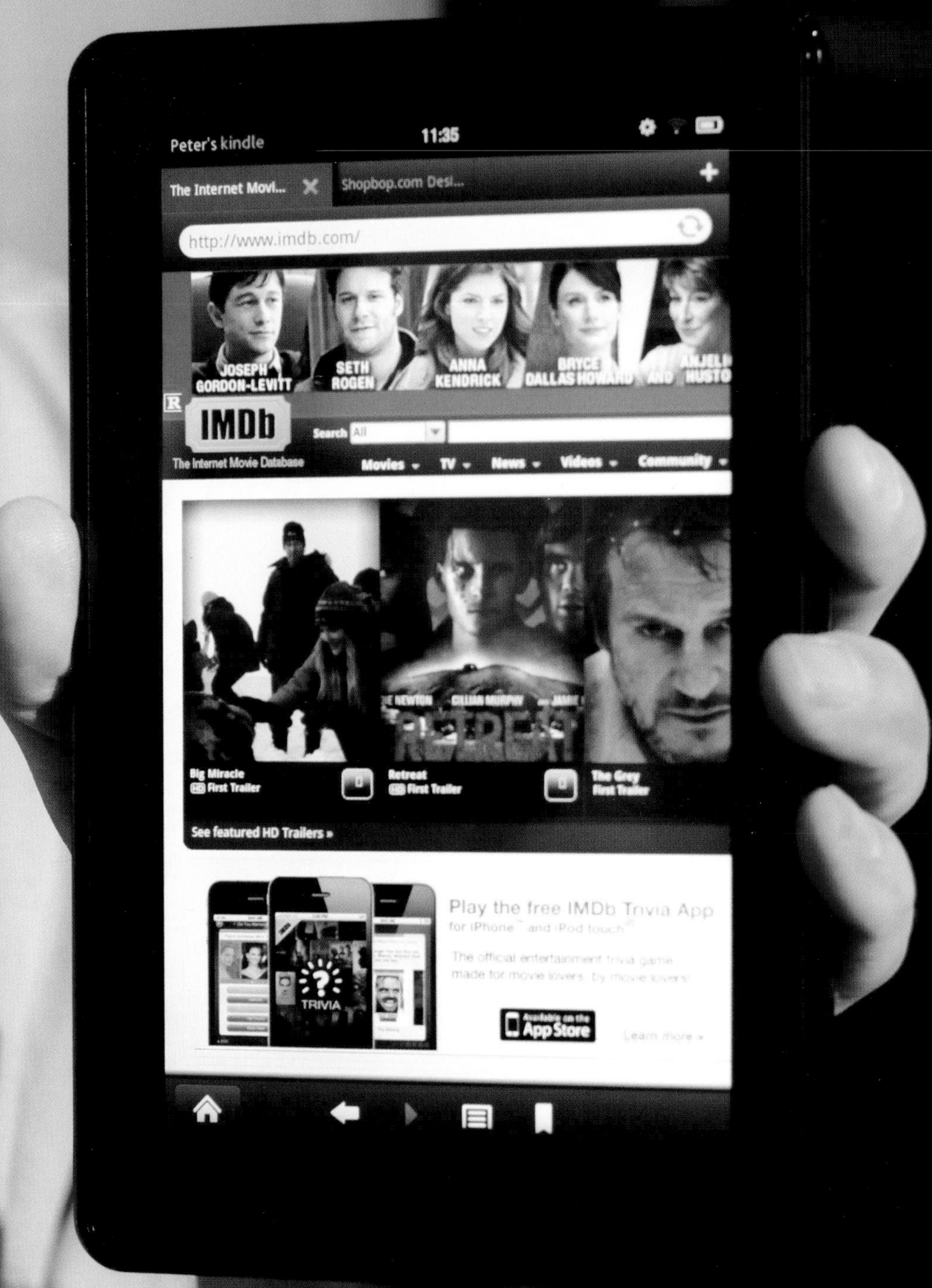

Users can surf the Web, watch movies, and play games on the Kindle Fire's 7-inch (17.8 cm) color display.

CHAPTER 2

Growing up, Bezos dreamed of becoming a cowboy or an astronaut.

THE YOUNG ENTREPRENEUR

Jeff Preston Jorgenson was born on January 12, 1964, in Albuquerque, New Mexico, to teenaged newlyweds. His mother, Jacklyn (Jackie) Gise Jorgenson, was 17 when she gave birth. Little is known about his biological father, who left the family when Jeff was 18 months old.

When Jeff was four, his mother remarried. Her new husband, Miguel (Mike) Bezos, adopted Jeff when he married Jackie and is the man Jeff considers to be his father. Mike Bezos, a Cuban refugee, arrived in the United States at 15 with nothing but a few items of clothing. He lived in an orphanage until he graduated from high school. Mike then worked his way through the University of Albuquerque. Once he earned an engineering degree, he worked for Exxon as a petroleum engineer. Mike and Jackie Bezos also had a daughter, Christina, born in 1969, and a son, Mark, who was born in 1970.

For much of his childhood, Jeff's second home was the Cotulla, Texas, ranch owned by his mother's family. His maternal grandfather, Lawrence Preston Gise, had worked for the US Defense Department designing missiles and nuclear technology before retiring to the ranch. Jeff spent summers at the ranch from age four to sixteen, helping with everything from cleaning livestock stalls to helping his grandfather repair farm equipment. As an adult, Jeff credits his time on the ranch with his "Pops" as helping to prepare him to be a successful entrepreneur. Years later, Jeff said:

One of the things that you learn in a rural area like that is self-reliance. People do everything themselves. That kind of self-reliance is something you can learn, and my grandfather was a huge role model for me: If something was broken, let's fix it. To get something new done you have to be stubborn and focused, to the point that others might find unreasonable.[1]

REAL FATHER

Jeff Bezos does not think often of the biological father who abandoned him and his mother when he was little more than a baby. "I've never been curious about him," he has said. "The only time it ever comes up is in the doctor's office when I'm asked for my medical history. I put down that I just don't know. My real father is the guy who raised me."[2]

TINKERING AROUND

Outside of the ranch, Jeff also showed signs of the intelligence and resourcefulness that later helped him build Amazon.com from the ground up. As a child, he enjoyed tinkering with electronics and trying to build new things from old parts. In a 2001 interview with the Academy of Achievement, Jeff recalled,

I was constantly booby-trapping the house with various kinds of alarms and some of them were not just audible sounds, but actually like physical

booby-traps. I think I occasionally worried my parents that they were going to open the door one day and have 30 pounds (13.6 kg) of nails drop on their head or something. Our garage was basically science fair central.[3]

Jeff's parents enrolled him in a special program for gifted children at an elementary school that was 20 miles (32 km) from home. There, he received his first exposure to a computer. At the time, personal computers were not available. After learning how to use the terminal that was on loan from a local company, Jeff and his classmates used it to play a *Star Trek* game.

By the time Jeff was a teenager, the Bezos family had moved

DESTINED FOR SUCCESS

Jeff showed signs of determination and problem-solving skills as a child, even as young as a toddler. When he was three, he decided he no longer wanted to sleep in his crib. After his mother refused, Jeff took apart the crib using a screwdriver. The plan worked—he got a real bed after that. As he grew, Jeff also took apart and put back together radios, tried to turn an old vacuum into a hovercraft, and built an alarm to keep his siblings out of his room.

Robert Spector, author of *Amazon.com: Get Big Fast*, wrote that Jeff seemed destined for success from an early age. "Bezos was precocious as an adolescent, willful, focused, and confident. As a youth league leader on the football field, he could remember his assignment and everyone else's as well. When his mother wouldn't buy him an Infinity Cube, he made his own. When he mapped out the scavenger hunt for his girlfriend's birthday, he demonstrated the kind of strategizing and long-term thinking that would form the direction of Amazon.com."[4]

to Miami, Florida, for Mike's job. In addition to studying hard on his way to becoming valedictorian of his class, Jeff worked as a fry cook at McDonald's. He made a point of studying the processes and innovations that made it a successful burger chain. The summer after graduation in 1982, Jeff and classmate Ursula Werner set out to go into business for themselves. They created the Dream Institute; the word *dream* was an acronym for "directed reasoning methods." It was a two-week summer camp for students in the fourth, fifth, and sixth grades. Students learned about space travel, fossil fuels, foreign policy, and other subjects meant to stretch young minds. In the informal setting of Jeff's bedroom, Jeff and Ursula tried to push their students to think creatively and apply what they had learned.

BELIEVING IN TECHNOLOGY

Bezos enrolled in Princeton University in 1982. He set out to study physics but soon discovered the subject was not one of his strengths. He did, however, have an unusual aptitude for computer programming. Between school years at Princeton, Bezos worked as a programmer for Exxon and for IBM's Santa Teresa Research Center in Silicon Valley.

Bezos graduated from Princeton University with summa cum laude honors.

He graduated in 1986 with a degree in computer science and engineering with a 4.2 grade point average in his degree program and a 3.9 overall.

Many options were open to Bezos after graduation. Several prestigious companies, including

Intel Corporation, AT&T, and Anderson Consulting tried to hire him. He also considered immediately starting his own business. However, he decided against this option in favor of gaining some experience in the business world first. He accepted a job offer from Fitel, a Wall Street start-up founded by the mother of a Princeton classmate.

A decade before the Internet took off, Fitel was trying to create a similar network, which they called Equinet. It linked computers between financial companies to facilitate stock trades. As a programmer, Bezos worked on a part of the system that let computers from different networks communicate with each other. His system worked so well that the first traders who tried it thought it was a hoax. In 1987, less than a year later, 23-year-old Bezos was promoted to associate director of

LOST OPPORTUNITY

While he was a rising star in the finance industry, Bezos still had his eye on entrepreneurship. In 1990, he almost had the chance to join with Halsey Minor, another young entrepreneur. Minor had been working on an internal network for Merrill Lynch. He hoped to expand the project to create a network in which subscribers could sign up to receive news stories based on their interests. Minor asked Bezos to partner with him. Merrill Lynch considered funding the company, but decided not to participate. Without funding, the project died before it started. However, Minor later founded the CNET news service, which made him a millionaire.

technology and business development—the second-ranking position at the small company.

A year later, he left Fitel to join Bankers Trust, another financial company. As the company's youngest vice president, Bezos oversaw the creation of its communication network, known as BTWorld. It allowed clients to track their investments remotely. Bezos had to convince bankers who firmly believed the firm should continue using paper reports to communicate with clients to try out this new system. Harvey Hirsch, who was Bezos's boss at the time, said:

> *He sees different ways of doing things and better ways of doing things. He told the naysayers, "I believe in this new technology, and I'm going to show you how it's going to work"—and he did. At the end of the day he proved them all wrong.*[5]

With that success under his belt, Bezos looked for a job outside the finance industry and ended up at D. E. Shaw in 1990. The company, founded in 1988 by former Columbia University computer science professor David Shaw, specialized in cutting-edge computerized stock-trading systems. Hiring was extremely selective—just 1 percent of applicants made the cut. Bezos quickly rose among

D. E. SHAW

In the late 1980s, computer software helped stock traders track prices so they knew when to buy and sell. Shaw's software automated the process even further, making trades more quickly than a human could achieve. The young company quickly built a reputation. The *Wall Street Journal* called Shaw's software "the vanguard of computerized selling," and *Fortune* magazine described it as "the most technologically sophisticated firm on Wall Street."[6]

those elite, becoming senior vice president by age 26. In that position, Bezos led a team of 24 people charged with looking for new opportunities for investment or technological advancement. Through his research, Bezos found an opportunity that was too good to pass up. +

Before starting D. E. Shaw, David Shaw was a faculty member in the Department of Computer Science at Columbia University.

CHAPTER 3

Bezos wanted to create an Internet catalog of books.

THE START-UP

In 1994, while investigating Internet business opportunities for D. E. Shaw, Bezos stumbled upon a startling statistic: Internet usage was growing at a rate of 2,300 percent per year. The figure was so high, Bezos questioned whether it could possibly be real. After reviewing the source and verifying that it was indeed accurate, he began looking for ways to harness that potential into a business model. "When something is growing by 2,300 percent a year, you have to move fast," Bezos said. "A sense of urgency becomes your most valuable asset."[1] The idea for an online retailer, the likes of which the world had not yet seen, began to take shape.

According to one story, Bezos sketched out his business plan as his wife, MacKenzie, drove a borrowed truck as they headed west. The real story was slightly less spontaneous than that. Bezos researched 20 different types of mail-order catalog businesses before deciding what to sell. One option he considered was music, but Bezos feared that the half a dozen major record companies might object to a newcomer who wanted to challenge the traditional business model.

Books quickly rose to the top of the list. Approximately 3 million

MACKENZIE BEZOS

Before he met his wife, Bezos had been known to say that the trait he most looked for in a woman was whether she could "get me out of a Third World prison."[2] By that, he meant he hoped to meet someone who was resourceful. MacKenzie Tuttle, an aspiring novelist, was a research assistant to author Toni Morrison while attending Princeton University. MacKenzie met Bezos at D. E. Shaw where she worked as a research associate. They married in 1993.

books were in print at the time, but there was no existing comprehensive catalogue from which to order. Therefore, Bezos could offer something that was not already available. The ability to catalogue and search books by title, author, publisher, or keyword made the prospect of an online retailer potentially more appealing than a physical bookstore. "With that huge diversity of products, you could build a store online that simply could not exist in any other way," Bezos explained his decision. "You could build a true superstore with exhaustive selection; and customers value selection."[3]

Furthermore, unlike the music industry, the book industry was already highly fragmented, including tens of thousands of publishers and many independent booksellers. Barnes & Noble and Borders, the two largest chain booksellers, accounted for one-quarter of the market in 1994. But Bezos expected to be able to compete with them through better selection and lower overhead. At the American Bookseller's Convention that year, Bezos furthered his research into the industry, finding out that wholesalers already maintained electronic lists of their inventories. All he needed to do was to compile the lists online, make them searchable, and enable customers to purchase books directly.

Still, starting the business was not an easy decision. As a senior vice president for D. E. Shaw—the company's youngest at age 30—Bezos already had a promising future and a high six-figure salary in New York City. Most start-ups fail, and his business was banking on an unknown variable. While the Internet was growing rapidly, it was not widely used, and whether people would be willing to make purchases over their computers was unproven. Bezos, however, knew he would regret not trying more than he would regret failing:

THE INTERNET BEFORE AMAZON.COM

The US Department of Defense experimented with creating a network that linked computers together in the 1960s. This led to Advanced Research Projects Agency Network (ARPANET), a precursor to the Internet. The first host-to-host ARPANET connection was made between UCLA and Stanford Research Institute on October 29, 1969. Other government agencies and academic institutions gradually began using the Internet to exchange information.

In 1988, the first commercial e-mail services started the move toward commercial and personal use of the Internet. In 1993, new software made navigating the Internet easier, opening the doors for people outside of the computer industry to use the Internet. In 1994, the University of Illinois released the first Web browser program, Mosaic, later renamed Netscape.

When Bezos began his plans for Amazon.com in 1994, almost no commerce was conducted online. Computer Literacy Bookshops started selling products through e-mail in 1991, then BookStacks Unlimited and WordsWorth. However, these were publications marketed to specialized groups.

I knew that when I was 80 I was not going to regret having tried this. I was not going to regret trying to participate in this thing called the Internet that I thought was going to be a really big deal. I knew that if I failed I wouldn't regret that, but I knew the one thing I might regret is not ever having tried. I knew that that would haunt me every day, and so, when I thought about it that way it was an incredibly easy decision.[4]

"He was one of the very first entrepreneurs to make a big bet on electronic commerce, quitting a promising career on Wall Street to move west and start Amazon when a lot of people didn't yet even know what the Internet was. He understood from the beginning that he wasn't just inventing a new and more efficient way for people to find books they wanted to buy but that he was also helping to define a fundamentally new way to conduct a consumer retail business. Indeed, Jeff's idea was just as revolutionary as when Sears, Roebuck started its mail-order catalog business a century earlier."[5]

—*Bill Gates*

Leaving the security of his job at D. E. Shaw behind, Bezos and his wife made the decision to move to Seattle, Washington. After flying to his home state of Texas to pick up a truck that was a gift from his father, they drove the rest of the way to their destination. They selected the Seattle area because of its proximity to a large book distribution warehouse and its large pool of technically skilled workers.

Convincing investors was another matter. Bezos was up front with his initial investors about the risk they were taking, reminding them that 95 percent of start-ups fail. He estimated that an Internet start-up had a one in ten chance of making it, but he had enough faith in his own idea that he predicted a 30 percent chance of success. This meant investors had a 70 percent chance of losing their money. Bezos borrowed from his own savings and received a $300,000 contribution from his parents. His father recalled that when he first heard of his son's idea, he did not know what the Internet even was. "We weren't betting on the Internet," his mother said. "We were betting on Jeff."[6] Other investors provided an additional $1 million.

Bezos incorporated the company in July 1994, under the name Cadabra. The company started out of the garage of the three-bedroom ranch home he and his wife rented in Bellevue, Washington. After seven months, Bezos changed the name to Amazon.com. Bezos constructed tables out of doors and two-by-four pieces of lumber, set up three large computer stations on them, and ran extension cords from every outlet in the house to

Amazon.com started out of the Bezos' garage in Bellevue, Washington.

power the computers. Amazon.com began with a staff of four people, which included Bezos and his wife, who helped out with accounting and office tasks. A veteran Silicon Valley programmer, Shel Kaphan, was one of the first people Bezos persuaded to join his start-up. As vice president of research and development, Kaphan was the primary architect of the original site. Paul Barton-Davis, a staff programmer for the University of Washington Computer Science Department, also came on board. Barton-Davis recalled being startled when he saw the makeshift office set up in Bezos's garage. "Boy, this really is Ground Zero," he remembered thinking.[7]

Since Internet commerce was new, Bezos, Kaphan, and Barton-Davis took steps to create trust with customers so they would feel comfortable supplying credit card numbers. Amazon.com instituted instantaneous e-mail order confirmations and a generous return policy and encrypted credit card numbers. To keep costs down, it would not keep its own inventory; instead, it purchased books through distributors as orders came in. The majority of Amazon.com's inventory came from Ingram Book Group, a company that sells large quantities of books to merchants.

With the Web site up and running, Bezos asked 300 friends and acquaintances to test it. The testing was a huge success. The Web site ran without problems

THE NAME

Bezos first chose the name Cadabra for his company after magicians' use of "abracadabra." However, he scratched the idea after someone misheard it as "cadaver." He selected Amazon.com, after the river in South America. Without referring to any specific product, the name left room for the company to grow. In 1999, *Time* magazine described it as the perfect choice. "The wild Amazon River, with its limitless branches, remains an ideal metaphor for a company that now sells everything from power tools to CDs, and is eagerly looking for new areas of expansion."[8]

across different computer systems, and the simple design was easy to use. One of the testers was David Shaw, Bezos's former employer. "When I saw the site, I said to myself, 'Wow. This is it,'" recalled Shaw.[9] +

Door desks became a staple in the Amazon.com offices.

CHAPTER 4

Bezos holds a copy of *Fluid Concepts and Creative Analogies*, the first book sold when Amazon.com opened in July 1995.

EARLY SUCCESS

On July 16, 1995, Amazon.com opened its virtual doors to the world. Instead of publicizing his new company through the media, Bezos simply asked the 300 testers to spread the word. A bell was set up to ring every time an order came in. At first, every time it sounded, the small staff erupted in cheers. But as orders poured in more rapidly than expected, the bell quickly became a nuisance. By the end of the first week, Amazon.com had sold approximately $12,000 worth of books. In the first month, orders came in from all 50 states and 45 countries. "Within the first few days, I knew this was going to be huge," Bezos said. "It was obvious that we were onto something much bigger than we ever dared to hope."[1]

EARLY AMAZON.COM

The Web site Amazon.com's first users saw in July 1995 was simple. The main page showed the company's first logo, an aqua-blue capital *A* with the top flattened and an image of a river rising up through the middle. The top of the page proclaimed, "Welcome to Amazon.com Books! Search one million titles. Enjoy consistently low prices."[2] It also contained navigational bars, informational text, and the image of one book cover that was spotlighted. Users could search by author, title, subject, publication date, and keyword.

The small staff was ill prepared for the site's immediate popularity. In the first few weeks, only a fraction of the orders coming in were shipped out to customers. As books came in from distributors, Bezos, his wife, and the few other employees packed, addressed, and shipped the orders. One computer was used to submit orders to book wholesalers and to process credit card transactions. According to Bezos, "Our business plan does not

When it launched in 1995, Amazon.com had a simpler appearance.

even begin to resemble what has actually happened." He also added,

> *I think one thing we missed was that the Internet was exclusively made up of early adopters at that time. So all the people online, even though it was a relatively small number compared with today, were those who liked to try new things.*[3]

Quickly, the company moved out of the garage and into 1,500 square feet (139 sq m) of office space in an industrial area of Seattle. Bezos constructed more desks out of doors, installed enough shelving to hold several hundred books ready to be shipped out, and purchased tables for packing orders. Holes were punched in the walls and ceiling to wire the network. Lauralee Smith, who worked as a special-orders clerk during this time, recalled her first impression of the office. "For a company that was as high tech and visionary as it was, the actual geographical location was a little uninspiring," Smith said. "It was a very shabby collection of offices that gave you the impression of being put together with duct tape."[4] The company was still operating on a shoestring for a time. Meetings were conducted at coffee shops, and the entire company had one e-mail address. Even Bezos answered some of the customer inquiries.

UNUSUAL ORDERS

When sales were low at the beginning, Amazon.com staffers were able to take notice of what customers were buying. For fun, they made lists of some of the most unusual or amusing titles that were purchased. One customer stumped everyone by purchasing 12 books containing the name Marsha in the title. Some of the other early titles that were purchased included: *Training Goldfish Using Dolphin Training Techniques*, *How to Start Your Own Country*, and *Life Without Friends*.

KEYS TO SUCCESS

Amazon.com had the advantage of timing when it launched. That year, the number of Internet users ballooned to 16 million people worldwide. It also had the advantage of being first; other major booksellers had not yet made a presence on the Web. However, because the idea of e-commerce was so new, Bezos took steps to increase booksellers' comfort level with online transactions. He offered several different options for customers to pay for their orders. If they did not want to complete their order through the Web site, they could submit credit card information through e-mail, finish the order over the phone, or mail a check. While half chose to give their credit card info over the phone, many trusted the Web site to handle transactions from the beginning.

Bezos also wanted to build confidence by making the site easy to use. The Web site did not require consumers to register until they were ready to complete a transaction and confirmed their orders. "Users were always reassured at each step that they were not making irreversible steps until they were ready to commit their orders," explained Kaphan, one of the initial developers. "I remember that next to the button to put something in the shopping basket, I put something like, 'you can always take it out later.'"[5]

The appearance of the site was also simple, in part because its developers were not graphic designers. But the simple layout meant pages loaded faster, even using the slow modems of the time, and the site was more easily navigable. Book publisher Tim O'Reilly commented on what made Amazon.com easier to use than other Web sites being created at the time:

> *A lot of people were spending a lot of time and energy making sites that were hard to use because they had*

LEARNING CURVE

As Amazon.com prepared to launch, the news reported about a hacker who stole thousands of credit card numbers, contributing to fears about online transactions. Programmer Paul Barton-Davis devised a system to keep customers' information safe. When transactions were processed, the information was put on a floppy disk, physically carried to and stored on a computer without Internet access. Anyone wanting to steal the information needed direct access to the disk or computer. This was called CC Motel, where "credit card numbers check in, but they don't check out."[6]

But the staff learned the site had a few kinks early on. Customers could put a negative number of books in their cart. This caused the company to credit their account for books that were never purchased.

They also discovered in testing there was no way to track individual customer activity or whether someone made more than one purchase. So programmers began tracking data using cookies, small files stored on a computer by a Web site, which retrieved customer shipping information and made recommendations based on previous purchases.

> *all kinds of fancy graphics. Amazon.com was so stripped down. They realized that what they were building was not a brochure; they were building an application.*[7]

One of Bezos's tactics was not new—discounting. Chain bookstores were in the practice of discounting prices on best-selling books to draw shoppers into the store. Amazon.com discounted the top 20 books by 30 percent, selling them at a loss, while marking down other titles by 10 percent. It also spotlighted a handful of books each day at 40 percent off their cover prices.

The company did no advertising during its first year, but it did receive some helpful buzz. Yahoo put the site on its What's Cool? list. Netscape promoted it on its What's New list, and the *Wall Street Journal* ran a front-page story. By October 1995, it was receiving approximately 100 orders per day. Within a year, Amazon.com reached 100 orders per hour.

"GET BIG FAST"

Within seven months, Amazon.com's growing staff outgrew its office space. Management moved to a separate office near downtown Seattle, and the warehouse expanded into the parking garage.

As Amazon.com grew, and it gained more attention, competitors started taking notice. Barnes & Noble responded quickly and had its own Web site running by May 1996.

Bezos was not to be deterred. He compared his approach to his pursuit of being valedictorian when he was in high school—he worked hard, avoided focusing on what his fellow students were doing, and came out on top of his class. Similarly, Bezos encouraged his staff to focus on improving the company and not dwell on the other companies that were set to become rivals. "I ask people to focus on our customers, not our competitors," Bezos said.[8] Another part of his strategy was to focus on growth over profits; he did not want to scrimp on marketing or infrastructure improvements for the sake of becoming profitable more quickly. The corporate mantra early on became, "Get big fast."

"THE BIGGEST BOOKSTORE ON EARTH"

Bezos liked to call Amazon.com "the biggest bookstore on earth" because it offered more than 1 million titles. However, because the company did not store inventory, it did not have those titles in stock. Even the distributors from which Amazon.com obtained books after orders were placed kept only approximately 300,000 titles in stock at a time.

"In terms of the number of books actually on hand at any one time, Amazon's competitors could have just as easily described it as one of the smallest bookstores on earth," observed Brandt.[10]

In 1997, Barnes & Noble attempted to sue Amazon.com for claiming that it was "the biggest bookstore on earth." The suit was settled out of court.

In 1996, Amazon.com's total sales reached $15.7 million—a 3,000 percent increase over its previous year. Losses also grew astronomically from $303,000 in 1995 to $6.2 million in 1996. In 1995, investors had still been skeptical about the long-term potential of something that seemed more like a novelty than a long-term company. But by 1996, investors were increasingly anxious to buy into the apparent promise of online commerce. "I would give them pieces of paper with our weekly sales growth, and they would say, 'Where do we send the check?'" Bezos recalled.[9]

At first, investors contributed approximately $30,000 apiece at a time when Bezos estimated the value of his company at approximately $6 million in 1995. But Amazon.com garnered attention from venture capitalists in 1996. Bezos met with several venture capitalists, including John Doerr. In 1996, Doerr offered $8 million, which was 13 percent of the company's valuation of $60 million. Bezos now had the capital to start making Amazon.com into the global behemoth of his dreams. +

Venture capitalist John Doerr invested $8 million in Amazon.com.

CHAPTER 5

Racks full of books at Amazon.com's Seattle distribution center in 1997

STAYING AHEAD

With more cash to work with, Bezos put a priority on growing Amazon.com quickly to stay ahead of competitors. "We are not profitable," he told the *New York Times* in 1997. He continued by saying:

We could be. It would be the easiest thing in the world to be profitable. It would also be the dumbest. We are taking what might be profits and reinvesting them in the future of the business.[1]

That did not mean Bezos spent money haphazardly; he still cut corners whenever possible. Even though the staff moved into a bigger office, for example, they still worked at desks constructed cheaply out of doors.

Instead, Bezos put the money into improving the site and service as well as developing new features. "Spotlight" was one of its first features. Each day, one book was highlighted on the front page. Initially, the selections were based on books Amazon.com had images and information for. Before long, editors were hired to produce more interesting content and write reviews to fill that slot. When publishers failed to provide enough information, editors even visited nearby bookstores to look at a book's dust jacket. Soon the Web site started making more personalized recommendations based on a customer's previous

"The site is so fast and responsive, it almost feels alive; it's thrilling to have every title in the language, and reader-produced reviews add a layer of egalitarian interactivity."[2]

—Time *review of Amazon.com*

interests, similar to what a knowledgeable staff member at a traditional bookstore might do.

The developers at Amazon.com soon came up with a way to let customers do some of this editorial work for themselves by creating ways for customers to review and rate products. The Web site also let customers post questions, which other customers could answer. For example, users could ask for or offer recommendations on what to read next. The feature not only inexpensively filled space on product pages with content, but it also helped Amazon.com build a reputation as a Web site that could be trusted to have the customers' best interests in mind.

Amazon.com became more than a place to buy books; it was a new way to socialize. To Bezos, it seemed people were interacting even more than they would if

POWER OF LUCK

Bezos admits he was not the only one to see the potential of Internet commerce or even the first. When asked why he was the one who was most able to capitalize on it, Bezos says luck played a large factor. "There are a lot of entrepreneurs. There are a lot of people who are very smart, very hard-working, very few ever have the planetary alignment that leads to a tiny little company growing into something substantial. So that requires not only a lot of planning, a lot of hard work, a big team of people who are all dedicated, but it also requires that not only the planets align, but that you get a few galaxies in there aligning, too. That's certainly what happened to us."[3]

they met in person at a bookstore. "I'm an outgoing person, but I'd never go into a bookstore and ask a complete stranger to recommend a book," Bezos said. "The semi-anonymity of the online environment makes people less inhibited."[4]

Some people were skeptical of the review feature when it was introduced. They did not understand why a bookseller would allow customers to share negative reviews of its products. They thought such a practice would hurt sales. There were also ways to misuse the system; people could write fake reviews to either damage or boost a product's sales. However, the interactive feature worked well enough that it not only has remained but other online commerce sites have copied it.

Marketing also became a priority as Amazon.com quickly dropped its original word-of-mouth strategy. In the first half of 1996, the company spent $340,000 on advertising in an effort to reach more customers outside those who were most familiar with the technology.

The company also made changes to streamline the shipping process. Early on, a book that was in stock with a distributor would be shipped within four days; the goal was to lessen that to 24 hours. To improve shipping time on special-order books—which initially took four to six weeks to ship—Amazon.com started keeping a handful of copies in the warehouse that would be restocked as they were sold. For these titles, Amazon.com employees scanned in an image of the cover and included a description and other available information on the product page. This program, called Publisher's Advantage, helped small independent publishers sell their books to a wider audience.

To improve shipping times across the board, Amazon.com began

1-CLICK SHOPPING

Shel Kaphan, head of software development, started looking for ways to further simplify ordering. Toward the end of 1997, one of his programmers, Peri Hartman, developed the system called 1-Click Shopping. Returning customers can choose to store information on their payment preferences, shipping location, and method of shipping in their account. To make a purchase, the user can click just one button and then see a confirmation that the order was submitted.

Amazon.com's decision to patent the process, granted in 1999, was controversial. The patent document merely explained the simple process of storing customer information and retrieving with a one-click ordering button located on a product page. Competitors thought the idea was too obvious and the patent was too broad, giving Amazon.com an unfair advantage. Barnes & Noble's version, rolled out in 1998, was called Express Lane 1-Click Ordering. Amazon.com filed suit against Barnes & Noble in October 1999. A district court upheld the patent in December 1999, and the two companies settled the suit out of court with undisclosed terms in 2002. Apple, on the other hand, paid a licensing fee to Amazon.com to use the technology for its online music store iTunes.

moving away from the inventory-free business model. Customers who could easily purchase a best seller from a nearby bookstore did not necessarily want to wait for a book to travel from the distributor to the warehouse, be packaged, and shipped to them. The Amazon.com warehouse started stocking best sellers, initially hundreds of copies at a time, but soon thousands.

In November 1996, the company leased 93,000 square feet (8,640 sq m) of space in Seattle to house the increasing inventory. The warehouse soon stored 200,000 books, ready to be shipped to customers. An additional warehouse opened in Delaware in 1997. It held an inventory of books from a dozen wholesalers as well as books obtained directly from 20,000 publishers. With the new warehouses, Amazon.com could achieve same-day shipping for 95 percent of the orders coming in for in-print books.

In late 1996 and early 1997, Bezos hired a handful of executives to help him run his growing company. They included executives from companies such as FedEx, Cinnabon, and Microsoft. David Risher was hired as vice president of product development and Joy Covey became Amazon.com's chief financial officer (CFO). Scott Lipsky, who

Amazon.com vice president David Risher previously worked as an executive at Microsoft and helped grow Amazon.com's profits.

previously worked for Barnes & Noble, also came onboard as vice president of business expansion.

GOING PUBLIC

On May 15, 1997, less than two years after Amazon.com started selling online, the company went public. This meant investors could buy and sell shares on the stock market. Amazon.com was traded on the NASDAQ under AMZN. The company did not hide the fact that it was not focused on making profits. Still, Amazon.com's stock initially sold at $18 per share, raising $54 million. The company was now valued at $429 million—more than seven times greater than the previous year. One year later, stock sold at $105 per share, and the company was valued at $5 billion. "Amazon had become the premier Internet commerce site," wrote Brandt. "With a two-year head start over the competition, huge brand name recognition, and growth in revenues, it had become an Internet star."[5]

Bezos continued streaming the money coming in toward expansion and innovation. Some features were added to personalize the experience. When customers

NOT FOR SALE

In late 1996, Barnes & Noble attempted to purchase Amazon.com. Bezos met with the bookstore chain's top two executives, Len and Steve Riggio. At that time, Bezos might have been able to sell his company for several hundred million dollars. While others might have seized this opportunity, he turned it down. He had plans to build his company into more than an online bookstore, and he wanted to see the plans through.

returned to the Web site, the home page now greeted them by name and made recommendations based on past purchases. The user could also view lists of best sellers and popular books. This helped simulate the experience of browsing that many bookstore companies enjoy. +

Joy Covey gets pointers at the Chicago Stock Exchange on November 19, 1997.

CHAPTER 6

Jeff Bezos in 1997

DIVERSIFYING AND EXPANDING

Once Amazon.com started maintaining its own warehouse inventory and obtaining books directly from publishers, it depended less on large book distributors. One distributor, Ingram Book Group, responded by starting up its own online store, but found it difficult to make inroads into the business Amazon.com had already established. In 1998, Ingram then set out to merge with Barnes & Noble. However, the Federal Trade Commission threatened to challenge the merger on the basis that it violated antitrust laws. Independent booksellers and some representatives of Congress also objected to the prospect. Soon, the deal was dropped, and Amazon.com maintained its dominance in the bookselling industry.

AMAZON.COM VERSUS BARNES & NOBLE

From 1995 to 1998, sales for Amazon.com doubled approximately every two and a half months, which amounted to 300 percent per year. In the period, Barnes & Noble's sales increased by 10 percent per year. Amazon.com brought in $375,000 per employee, more than three times the per-employee revenue of Barnes & Noble. For every dozen times Amazon.com turned over its inventory, its chain-store competitor did so just once.

BEYOND BOOKS

Bezos had plans to break into other industries—starting with movies. Bezos's first action, in April 1998, was to purchase the Internet Movie Database (IMDb), a site that posts information and reviews about movies and television shows.

Next, Bezos decided to sell music. In 1994, when Bezos was deciding what to sell, music ranked second to books. Debuting in June 1998, Amazon.com's music store offered 125,000 CDs, approximately ten times the number of titles offered by a traditional music store. Similar to its bookstore offerings, Amazon.com offered steep discounts, customer reviews, recommendations, lists, and 1-Click Ordering. Additionally, customers could sample short audio clips before purchasing.

Once again, Bezos encountered skepticism. The *Wall Street Journal* called the expansion beyond books "risky," speculating that Amazon.com would "dilute its reputation as a destination for book lovers."[1] Unlike when he went into the book business, Bezos faced existing competition online. CDNow.com and n2k.com had sold music for several years and decided to merge in October 1998, to better compete with Amazon.com. Bezos stayed confident, however, that his strategy would prevail:

> *This is not a winner-take-all kind of business. Online commerce is a big arena. It's not going to be the case where you have one company who dominates this marketplace. You are going to have a leader, and clearly, we want to be that leader in every area that we enter into. And the way you*

Amazon.com purchased the Internet Movie Database in 1998.

become that leader is to focus obsessively on the customer experience.[2]

The strategy worked. Amazon.com's music store sold $14 million in the first four months, outselling CDNow.com. The success in selling music, in addition to the general fervor over Internet businesses, caused Amazon.com's stock to soar on July 6 to $139.50.

ACQUISITIONS

When Amazon.com started selling DVDs and videos in November 1998, it used IMDb to advertise.

Within two months, Amazon.com had become the largest seller of movies on the Internet.

Bezos started acquiring other Internet companies, some of which were not commerce sites. PlanetAll was an online address and appointment book that could send e-mail reminders—the first service of its kind. Junglee helped shoppers compare prices for products available on different Web sites. While it could potentially send customers away from Amazon.com for a better price, Bezos saw the potential of such a service to create goodwill. He also had a long-term plan to turn it into zShops, which eventually became Amazon Marketplace. This allowed third parties to sell products through Amazon's site, with Amazon.com receiving a commission.

Some people were skeptical that encouraging customers to buy products from other companies would backfire on Amazon.com. Bezos steadfastly asserted that the more people he could attract to

FIRST ONLINE CHRISTMAS

Online shopping had its first major impact on holiday shopping habits in 1998. More than \$3.5 billion worth of goods were sold online during that holiday season. Popular online purchases included books; computer hardware, software, and accessories; CDs; and movies. Approximately 1.7 million new customers made purchases on Amazon.com from November 17 to December 31. The company quickly hired hundreds of new employees to field the orders, but even then some orders were not shipped in time for Christmas.

the Web site through this kind of service, the better off his company would be. He also considered that if people researched products on Amazon.com and then bought them elsewhere, he could start charging a yearly club membership fee. This would help him lower prices and retain club members. Amazon.com has not charged a club membership fee, but the idea of selling others' products paid off. In 2010, more than a third of the company's revenue was estimated to have come from Amazon Marketplace.

ASSOCIATES PROGRAM

The Associates Program allowed other businesses or Web sites to link directly to Amazon.com products. If someone purchased a product through one of those links, the associate would receive a commission of 5 to 15 percent. The ability to link to material on specialized topics cemented the reputation of Amazon.com's large inventory. It also helped Bezos minimize competition from companies that otherwise might have started their own specialty bookstores. One former Amazon.com employee disagreed that the arrangement was mutually beneficial. "The idea is not for someone to keep going back to that other site and buy books through that channel every time. It's to get a new customer and keep him."[3]

Amazon.com drew criticism for patenting this idea because the practice of linking to products was not entirely new. However, Bezos never took the issue to court even as other companies developed their own affiliate programs.

SPREADING TO INTERNATIONAL PUBLISHERS

Bezos also started expanding globally. At first, he tried working out a deal to join with

German publisher Bertelsmann AG, which wanted a 50 percent stake in Amazon.com's European business. When the deal did not go through, Bertelsmann joined with Barnes & Noble.

In 1998, Amazon.com acquired online bookstores based in Great Britain and Germany. They were relaunched as Amazon.co.uk and Amazon.co.de. New distribution centers were opened to serve these countries. The Internet was slower to catch on overseas; Europe's population was less than half the number of people already online in the United States. Amazon.com also had to work within local laws, such as those prohibiting discounting in Germany. However, the ventures were successful enough that Bezos continued expanding Amazon.com to more countries.

Amazon.com also distanced itself further from book distributors. In 1999, five new warehouses were constructed around the United States, increasing Amazon.com's capacity tenfold. Bezos outfitted the centers with the latest technology, including tracking systems, bar-code readers, radio transmitters, and conveyor belts. "This is the fastest expansion of distribution capacity in peacetime history," Bezos said at the time.[4] +

Amazon.com acquired and relaunched online bookstores based in Germany and Britain in 1998.

CHAPTER 7

Known for being funny and sociable as Amazon.com's CEO, Bezos was named *Time* magazine's Person of the Year in 1999.

RIDING HIGH

Throughout 1999, Bezos and Amazon.com acquired or invested in a new company or product area almost on a monthly basis. Amazon.com started adding more to its selection, including toys, electronics, software, and video games. Acquisitions included Drugstore.com, music seller eNiche.com, MusicFind, HomeGrocer.com, rare books specializer Bibliofind, retailer Accept.com, half of sporting goods retailer Gear.com, and Alexa Internet, a company that tracked people's browsing habits. After unsuccessfully trying to buy online greeting card company Blue Mountain, Amazon.com created its own line of greeting cards.

Some of these attempts panned out better than others. The newly created Amazon Auctions, for example, simply could not compete with the already well-established eBay site. In 1999, eBay had 3 million customers and was making a profit. While eBay facilitated sales between individuals, Amazon.com's auction site featured items being sold by anyone, including larger merchants. To protect buyers, Amazon.com guaranteed sales up to $250 and created a rating system for transactions. Product pages throughout the rest of the site

ONLINE PRIVACY

One practice that led to some concerns was Amazon.com's focus on personalizing the Web site and making individually tailored recommendations. It based these actions on previous purchases and demographic information. Some people objected to the fact that this large corporation was tracking and using large amounts of personal information. Amazon.com responded to complaints by making privacy statements available, detailing what information was being stored and what was being done with it.

promoted the auctions. In June 1999, Amazon.com joined with a 250-year-old art house, Sotheby's Holdings, to create sothebys.amazon.com. The site auctioned off art, antiques, and collectibles that were less expensive than the ones Sotheby sold in its traditional auctions. But the partnership lasted less than a year because it could not compete with eBay's presence in the market. The rest of Amazon.com's auction service merged with zShops to form Amazon Marketplace, which sells used and new items.

PERSON OF THE YEAR

In just four years, Bezos's company had transformed from a garage start-up to a global empire. In recognition of these efforts, *Time* magazine named Jeff Bezos its Person of the Year in 1999. At age 35, Bezos became the fourth-youngest person given that honor.

In his article, Joshua Quittner describes the experience of visiting one of the company's new distribution warehouses in rural Coffeyville, Kansas. Strategically, similar warehouses had been built in states with low or no sales taxes. Unlike other companies' distribution centers, which shipped products to retail stores, these were designed

Sotheby's president Diana Brooks with Bezos

specifically to deliver products directly to customers. The 850,000-square foot (79,000 sq m) facility in Coffeyville was only 10 percent full at the time Quittner visited, but Bezos envisioned filling it with almost every type of product imaginable—from home appliances to food products. He also planned to sell services through the Web site, such as banking or travel.

While the article trumpeted its honoree's successes, it also expressed doubts that were forming about whether what Bezos envisioned was possible. While Amazon.com was, in many product categories, either getting there first or surpassing those who had, more and more competitors were trying to get a piece of the online pie. Some hosted specialty stores, selling only pet products or luxury items or some other specific type of good; others aimed to be the online equivalent of a mall. Existing chains, such as Wal-Mart, were getting ready to move online and had the advantage of name recognition. Meanwhile, Amazon.com was accumulating more and more debt as it grew. "It's incredibly risky," Quittner wrote of Amazon.com's plans to expand into every product category possible. "How elastic is the Amazon brand name? How much can you stretch it until it simply explodes and becomes meaningless to consumers? And how long can the money hold out?"[1]

AMAZON ON THE GO

In October 1999, Amazon.com became the first retailer to create a simplified site that could be accessed using handheld wireless devices, such as phones. The site was named Amazon.com Anywhere. "If customers are in the car and they hear a song they like, they can look it up and purchase it," said Warren Adams, director of product development for Amazon.com at the time. "In our mind, this is a cash register in every pocket."[2]

QUESTIONS ABOUT THE FUTURE

As Amazon.com grew to sell more products in more places, the company still was not making profits. It lost $720 million in 1999 and had $2 billion in debt. Still, through 1999, Amazon.com's stock continued climbing even as some financial experts warned that it was overvalued. The stock fluctuated between $100 and more than $300 per share.

Skeptics warned that Amazon.com could not sustain itself as it continued piling up debt without bringing in profits. In March 1999, Peter de Jonge wrote in the *New York Times*:

> *For all its all-nighters and tattooed punks humping books in the distribution center and golden retrievers wandering the halls in the corporate office, Amazon.com is a $20 billion, 2,100-employee company built on the thin membrane of a bubble, and this brings a manic precariousness to the place that no amount of profitless growth can diminish.*[3]

Amazon.com was not the only company in this boat. As technology stocks soared across the board, some people began questioning whether the stocks had been inflated beyond their real values. They compared the lofty values given to technology stocks to a bubble that would soon burst with potentially disastrous results. Others thought a new kind of economy had arrived. *Forbes* publisher Rich Karlgaard wrote an opinion piece that was published in the *Wall Street Journal*:

What really is going on? Are we hearing the trumpets and heralds of the grandly anticipated New Economy? Or is it the carnival bark of a stock-market sucker bet? . . . The answer is resoundingly: both. Yes, Amazon and Yahoo and the like are laughably overvalued. But, yes, Amazon and Yahoo are bullet-proof evidence that we live in a New Economy.[4]

PRODUCT PLACEMENT

Historically, publishers have paid traditional bookstores to prominently feature certain books. However, when Amazon.com was caught allowing something similar, it became a public relations problem. In 1999, the *New York Times* exposed the fact that the company had been accepting payments of $10,000 to offer special treatment to a book, including an author interview, prominent placement on the home page, and other perks. Stephen King's *Bag of Bones*, for example, was conspicuously featured on the best-seller page and featured on a list of books editors had deemed "destined for greatness." Customers also received e-mail notifications counting down to the release date.

Mary Morouse, vice president for purchasing, defended the practice and pointed out that editors could exclude books that did not merit the attention. In response to negative press and customer complaints, Bezos made it the company's policy to disclose when publishers had paid for placement. He claimed to be the first retailer to make that information available.

Others were more confident that Amazon.com's daring strategy would pay off. Holly Becker, a stockbroker for Salomon Smith-Barney said, "We firmly believe that Wall Street will look back on these growing pains and realize management's foresight in developing one of the smartest strategies in business history."[5]

By the end of 1999, Amazon.com's staff had increased to 5,000 employees. Revenues for that year were $1.5 billion, while expenses totaled $2 billion. To finance the company, Bezos depended on the strong showing of its publicly traded stock as the company was still operating at a loss. Amazon.com was coming off another successful holiday season; it had been the top shopping choice for 42 percent of online shoppers. Amazon.com had become a household name, with more than half of US citizens recognizing it.

In 2000, the company announced it was changing its logo. The original logo—a capital

FOLLOWING AMAZON.COM

The success of Amazon.com caused other companies to try to establish an online presence, afraid of being left behind. General Motors president and chief operating officer G. Richard Wagoner Jr. explained why his company went online in 1999. "We look at companies like Amazon.com, which we hadn't heard of three or four years ago and look at the impact they've had, and we say, this is something we need to get our arms around," said Wagoner. "We want to play aggressively in this business and we want to win."[6]

letter *A* with an image of a flowing river running up through it—was replaced with the word "Amazon," with an arrow that curved from the *A* to the *z*. It was meant to suggest that any product, starting with any letter of the alphabet, could be found on Amazon.com's site—even if Amazon.com did not sell it itself.

Indeed, through acquisitions of other companies, Amazon.com had started selling everything from books and music to electronics and games. But while it had achieved quick dominance in books, music, and movies, it had stiff competition in some areas. In the toy category, eToys was beating Amazon.com, and Blue Mountain still led Amazon.com in the greeting card business. As the new millennium approached, many wondered what the future held for this online giant. +

With its acquisitions of other companies, Amazon.com was starting to offer everything from A to Z.

CHAPTER 8

The dot-com bubble impacted Amazon.com and other technology companies.

SURVIVING AND THRIVING

As Internet companies multiplied and grew in the last few years of the twentieth century, stock prices rose based on confidence in future profits and excitement over the new technology. Many start-ups followed Bezos's philosophy of emphasizing growth over profits. But there was a limit to how much Amazon.com and other companies could grow without a business plan that would lead to revenues. In 2000, the stock values of Internet and technology companies started falling drastically across the board as investors realized the actual worth of those companies did not live up to expectations. Many went out of business; others rushed to cut costs in hopes of becoming profitable. This period of rapid growth followed by collapse in the technology sector became known as the dot-com bubble.

Even the mighty Amazon.com was not immune to the burst of the dot-com bubble. In mid-1999, executives began worrying when the tone of conversations with Wall Street investors started changing. They asked more serious questions about aspects of the business that would contribute to its long-term viability, such as operational efficiencies. They were increasingly uncomfortable with the fact that in five years Amazon.com had racked up $2 billion in debt and $1.72 billion in losses. "It's time for these guys to start performing like real retailers," retail analyst Gene Alvarez said. "The Internet panache has worn off and now it's time to start performing."[1]

Amazon.com workers fill Christmas orders in a Seattle distribution center in December 1999.

MAKING CHANGES

At an employee meeting in December 1999, Bezos announced a plan to focus more on profits. At the start of 2000, Amazon.com reduced its workforce by 150 employees and brought in new executives to rein in its expenses. In spite of these efforts, Amazon.com's stock plummeted along with other companies. It lost 90 percent of its value from the end of 1999 to the end of 2000. Having once surpassed $300 per share, it bottomed out at $15.

In an effort to reverse the tailspin, Bezos embarked on a public relations campaign in which he emphasized Amazon.com's determination to turn a profit. In December 2000, he told a reporter with *Fortune* magazine that the company had set an internal goal to achieve a profit by a specific, publically undisclosed date. He showed the reporter an e-mail that had been sent to the approximately 7,000 employees of the company:

> *We're putting a stake in the ground: We're going to become profitable. That's right: We're aiming to have sales of $5 billion produce $1 billion in gross profits, and achieve solid operating profitability by [Christmas of 2001].*[2]

Newly focused on the bottom line, Bezos started looking for additional ways to cut costs. He discontinued his least profitable business ventures and focused more on creating realistic budgets for every department. Managers were required to take financial training courses and set time lines for achieving revenue goals.

SLOW RECOVERY

Before the end of the 2000, some promising signs of a comeback began appearing. Losses were down for Amazon.com, and gross profit margins were up by more than a quarter. Its stock, however, was still performing weakly.

While revenues became increasingly important, Amazon.com still had room to grow, and it found ways to survive the bubble burst. In 2000, it added new product lines, including outdoor furniture, health and beauty products, and kitchenware. Companies that Amazon.com had invested in, such as living.com and Audible.com, paid large sums of money to be linked to Amazon.com's home page.

In 2001, Amazon.com cut costs more drastically by another workforce reduction. This time 1,300 people—15 percent of

STAYING FOCUSED

While Amazon.com's stock wobbled up and down in 2000 and 2001, Bezos kept his cool—at least publicly. He told interviewers that he was used to working amid skepticism and that his current obstacles were nothing compared to what he faced in 1994. While his strategy shifted, he asserted that his focus on customer service remained the same. "The smart people we have here don't sit around thinking about what the stock market will do. We sit around trying to figure out what the customer likes, and we give them that. . . . We have to invent on their behalf."[3]

its employees—lost their jobs. A customer service center in Seattle and a warehouse in Georgia were closed. In turn, the cost-cutting measures helped Amazon.com keep prices low to increase sales. By the end of 2001, strategies to cut costs and increase revenues were paying off.

In January 2002, Bezos announced that his company had reached its goal of turning a profit for the first time ever. In the fourth quarter, it eked out a narrow profit of $5 million. The day after the announcement, Amazon.com's stock rose by more than 40 percent. On more stable ground, Amazon.com continued

DOT-COM CASUALTIES

Not all companies survived the dot-com crash as well as Amazon.com. Some companies invested in creating a solid business plan; others failed to attract customers.

Online grocer Webvan spent millions of dollars on infrastructure in cities across the country but was unable to attract enough customers to survive.

Pets.com spent huge amounts of money on advertising—including a Super Bowl commercial and a float in the Macy's Thanksgiving Day parade—but never persuaded pet owners to buy supplies online. Because of shipping costs for items such as pet food or cat litter, it lost money on most of its sales.

Kozmo.com delivered movies, snacks, and other small items in metro areas within an hour. Customers loved the convenience, but the company soon discovered that providing free delivery for such small orders was too costly to sustain.

Flooz.com tried to create an online currency alternative to credit cards. It raised $35 million from investors, but the idea never caught on with the public.

Bezos and Borders Group president and CEO Greg Josefowicz

growing. In 2002, the company expanded into Canada and added office products and apparel to its product selection.

Bezos also found a new way to make money. He started using his company's proven technology to build and maintain Web sites for other large companies. Amazon.com partnered with vendors such as Target, Toys"R"Us, Circuit City, and Borders.

These deals tended to be beneficial for both parties. Toys"R"Us, for example, had been struggling with Web site crashes and shipping errors. In exchange for helping it solve these problems, Amazon.com no longer had to pay up front for a large inventory of toys, which were provided by Toys"R"Us. The arrangement ended in 2007 when Amazon.com began selling toys from other merchants.

In 2002, the company introduced Amazon Web Services. Over the next several years, Amazon.com built data centers around the globe to house large computer systems. For a fee, users can run software or store data on Amazon's servers and access these through the Internet. This is called cloud computing. Many companies use such services to avoid paying up front to build their own data centers. Instead, they can pay as they go for only as much computer

SIX CORE VALUES

While navigating both the dot-com crash and expansion, Bezos emphasized Amazon.com's Six Core Values. These are:

- customer obsession
- ownership
- bias for action
- frugality
- high hiring bar
- innovation

"Our vision," Bezos said, "is the world's most customer-centric company. The place where people come to find and discover anything they might want to buy online."[4]

power and storage as they are using. For example, as of 2011, Netflix did not have enough computing capability to support its popular video streaming service. So Netflix paid Amazon.com to store and stream some of its content on its servers. Industry analysts estimated that Amazon Web Services would make $2.5 billion for Amazon by 2014. +

AMAZON PRIME

In 2005, Amazon.com introduced Amazon Prime. For a subscription fee of $79 per year, customers receive free, two-day shipping on eligible items with no limit and no extra fees. Bezos considered it a gamble at first, comparing the service to an all-you-can-eat buffet. Prime users did end up buying more products, but the increase in sales offset the costs to the company of providing the two-day shipping. On average, Prime customers spend 130 percent more than other Amazon.com customers. Increasing the number of fulfillment centers has helped Amazon.com improve shipping times and lower its shipping costs.

Amazon.com launched Amazon Web Services in 2002.

CHAPTER 9

Jeff and MacKenzie Bezos in 2010

AMAZON TODAY

Fifteen years after Amazon.com sold its first book from the Bezos's garage in 1995, Amazon.com continued to thrive. Its stock rose by more than 10,000 percent between 1996 and 2010. In 2010, the company invested $175 million in LivingSocial.com, a Web site that offers daily deals and discounts, and continued developing its Amazon Web Services. Steven Levy of *Wired* magazine wrote in 2011, "People are slowly beginning to realize just how much of the Web is powered by Amazon's cloud services."[1]

Meanwhile, several companies, such as Barnes & Noble and Borders, have struggled to compete with Amazon.com's dominance. Borders closed all of its nearly 400 stores in 2011. Barnes & Noble has had some success with its Nook e-reading devices, but struggled in its paper book sales. Barnes & Noble's stock dropped 29 percent between 1996 and 2010.

IMPACT OF A GIANT

Following the introduction of the first Kindle in November 2007, publishers made approximately 10 percent of their revenues from the sale of e-books by the end of 2010. An estimated 20 percent of books were sold as e-books. This seems like a success for Amazon.com and others who entered the e-book business. However, because Amazon.com sold most digital titles at $9.99, less than what publishers asked for, Amazon.com sold many e-books at a loss. Publishers pressured Amazon.com to increase its

Bezos introduced the Kindle DX in 2009.

prices, fearing customers would become accustomed to cheap e-books and would not be willing to pay more. For these reasons, Amazon.com raised prices on many titles in 2010.

Amazon.com used this strategy of lowering prices on other products as well, incurring short-term losses on low-priced products to build its customer base. This strategy, however, has had repercussions on the publishing industry. Publishers have felt pressure to lower their prices on physical and digital books. In some cases, if they do not, Amazon.com removes their books from the site or removes the "add to shopping cart" button on the product pages. Many have given in because they cannot afford to lose Amazon.com's customers.

As publishers' profit margins are squeezed, they may focus more on books that are likely to be best sellers, leading to less variety in what is available. "Clearly, the deep, deep discounting of both physical and digital books is bad for consumers, publishers, retailers," said Oren Teicher, CEO of the American Booksellers Association. "You end up with fewer choices. The evidence is clear that if you keep discounting the product, there will be less product."[2] Bezos has countered that with lower prices and the convenience of e-readers, people are able to buy more books.

FOCUS ON CUSTOMERS

While Bezos has repeatedly said that he puts his customers first, others have criticized his approach. According to Oren Teicher, CEO of the American Booksellers Association, Bezos "does not really care about books. He uses books as loss leaders to sell everything else. He's acquiring customers to sell them whatever he can ultimately sell them. He has become the expert at marketing [other products] to customers once they've got them on the site."[3]

Amazon.com has also made it easier for authors to bypass publishers entirely. Anyone can self-publish through CreateSpace, a company owned by Amazon.com. CreateSpace prints books only after they are ordered. Another option for aspiring authors is to upload a manuscript into Kindle format for Kindle users to purchase. Amazon.com lets authors keep 70 percent of the royalties for self-published electronic books. Barnes & Noble once again followed in Amazon.com's footsteps with a similar service called PubIt! for the Nook.

SURVIVAL OF BOOKSTORES

While some chain bookstores have had difficulty competing with Amazon.com, independent bookstores are making a comeback. In 2009, membership in the American Booksellers Association increased for the first time in 15 years. As Bezos predicted in 1998, sometimes customers still want the experience of shopping in a physical bookstore.

> *What you're going to see—and it's happening already—is that physical bookstores will become even-nicer places to be," Bezos said. "They are going to have more sofas, better lattes, nicer people working there. Good bookstores are the community centers of the 20th century. That's the basis on which they're going to compete.*[4]

Suzanna Hermans, co-owner of independent bookstore Oblong Books in Rhinebeck, New York, told *USA Today* her bookstore emphasizes service and is a popular gathering spot in the community. "Bookstores help create community for people in the places where they live," Hermans said. "People may think they can live online, but in reality they live in real towns and cities, and physical bookstores help to enrich those places."[5]

Some may think that increasingly easy self-publishing could pose a threat to the traditional way of authors working with publishers to market and distribute books. "The only really necessary people in the publishing process now are the writer and the reader," said Russell

Grandinetti, vice president of books for Amazon.com. "Everyone who stands between those two has both risk and opportunity."[6]

NEW TECHNOLOGIES

As in the years leading up to the announcement of the first Kindle, Bezos can be very secretive about what his company plans to do next. But glimpses of Amazon's future plans can be seen in what patents it has applied for. In 2008, the company applied to patent a process by which a customer would place an order using body movements—such as holding up a number of fingers to indicate quantity or nodding one's head to confirm a request. The patent is titled Movement Recognition as Input Recognition, but industry insiders call it the I-Nod patent.

Another innovation in the works is a system that would let people prevent unwanted gifts from arriving. People could set rules, such as "no clothes

SUPPORTING WRITERS

While it has strayed far from its roots as just a bookseller, Amazon.com's Web site still proclaims, "A love of reading and an appreciation for the people who create great books is part of our DNA."[7] To support the writing community, the company provides grants to nonprofit groups that encourage the art of writing. Awards have gone to the Alliance for Young Artists and Writers, the Artist Trust, the Asian-American Writers' Workshop, the Center for the Art of Translation, Girls Write Now, the Loft Literacy Center, Poets and Writers, and dozens more.

with wool" or "convert any gift from Aunt Mildred to a gift certificate."[8] The company submitted a patent application for this process in 2010. While it is unclear what these patents will lead to, it is clear Amazon.com plans to continue innovating.

Bezos has also branched off into several new technologies. In February 2011, Amazon.com began offering a video-on-demand service to compete with Netflix Instant. Later, Amazon.com made it part of its video streaming library available for no extra cost to Amazon Prime subscribers, who pay an annual fee for unlimited two-day shipping of eligible products. In March 2011, Amazon.com introduced the Cloud Drive file storage service. Bundled with Cloud Drive is the Cloud player, a music streaming application. Cloud Drive lets users store up to five gigabytes of music or other files on Amazon's servers for free, to be accessed from anywhere.

And Amazon.com is still growing. At the beginning of 2011, the company had approximately 37,900 employees—a 45 percent increase from one year earlier. Over the course of the year, it opened 17 new fulfillment centers. The spending spree meant low single-digit profit margins. But Bezos was keeping to his original strategy—investment in growth would pay off in the long term.

While e-book prices have gone up, prices for the device have gone down. As of the beginning of 2012, a basic Kindle could be purchased for $79. The Kindle Touch was priced at $99, a Kindle Touch 3G cost $149, and Kindle Keyboard 3G was priced at $139. The Kindle Fire was priced at $199, half the price of the original Kindle.

Because of the expense of manufacturing the devices' screens, industry experts have speculated that Amazon.com is selling the new Kindle Fires at a loss. However, once people own the device, they are likely to purchase content and services for it. "Amazon Kindle products might be the best salesman for Amazon products," one reviewer wrote.[9]

"As you sit there reading, say, a literate and charming book review from Bangladesh, the real power of the Amazon brand comes home. It is a site that is alive with uncounted species of insight, innovation and intellect. No one predicted that electronic shopping could possibly feel this alive. If it is a sign of an e-world yet to come, a place in which technology allows all of us to shop, communicate and live closer together, then Jeff Bezos has done more than construct an online mall. He's helped build the foundation of our future."[10]

—*Joshua Cooper Ramo,* Time

INTO THE FUTURE

Outside of Amazon.com, Bezos has been working on one of his longtime goals since 2000: making the experience of spaceflight more affordable. He founded the company Blue Origin to work on the technology and employed former NASA engineers and other scientists specializing in the field. The company's motto is the Latin phrase *grandatim, ferociter* (step by step, courageously). Blue Origin's first goal is to build a spacecraft that can affordably send people to the edge of outer space to see Earth and stars from that vantage point and bring them back to Earth safely.

It is a difficult goal, one that might take years, even decades, to achieve. Some people doubt that commercial spaceflight will ever be a viable business. But as with Amazon.com, Bezos refuses to be deterred when faced with skepticism.

"Bezos will stop to rest when he's dead," wrote Brandt. "Until then, he's simply going to keep working, reinventing, trying new things, striving to reach the stars. Someday he may just get there."[11] +

Bezos received an Innovation Award in September 2011 from *Economist* magazine for developing the Kindle and popularizing handheld e-books.

TIMELINE

1964

Jeff Bezos is born as Jeff Preston Jorgenson on January 12 in Albuquerque, New Mexico.

1990

Working for D. E. Shaw, Bezos is promoted to senior vice president at age 26.

1993

Bezos marries MacKenzie Tuttle, a research associate at D. E. Shaw and aspiring novelist.

1996

Amazon.com abandons the inventory-free business model. It starts filling warehouses with books to fill orders faster.

1997

Amazon.com goes public in May, trading on the NASDAQ as AMZN.

1997

In September, Amazon.com introduces 1-Click Shopping.

IMPACT ON SOCIETY

When Amazon.com launched in 1995, the Web site's customer base quickly grew as people grew accustomed to buying products over the Internet. With Bezos's emphasis on growth over profits, Amazon.com quickly grew to branch into many product areas. Amazon.com pioneered much of the technology that is used for online shopping, including the ability to securely transmit payments over the Internet, the automated practice of making recommendations based on past purchases, and the convenience of one-click ordering. The introduction of the Kindle changed the way people read books.

QUOTE

"There are a lot of entrepreneurs. There are a lot of people who are very smart, very hardworking, very few ever have the planetary alignment that leads to a tiny little company growing into something substantial. So that requires not only a lot of planning, a lot of hard work, a big team of people who are all dedicated, but it also requires that not only the planets align, but that you get a few galaxies in there aligning, too. That's certainly what happened to us."

—Jeff Bezos

GLOSSARY

antitrust
Opposing monopolies, especially with a view to maintaining and promoting competition.

architect
A person who designs a Web site or program.

browser
A computer program that helps a user locate Web sites on the Internet.

capital
Accumulated wealth especially as used to produce more wealth.

developer
A person who creates computer software.

digitized
Words or images converted into data that can be stored electronically.

dot-com
An online business or commercial Web site.

e-commerce
The buying and selling of goods through the Internet.

electrode
A conductor device (as a transistor) through which current enters or leaves an electric or electronic device.

entrepreneur
A person who starts a business.

hovercraft
A vehicle that is supported above the ground by a cushion of air produced by downwardly directed fans.

modem
An electronic device that transmits data from one computer to another via phone lines.

network
A system of computers, peripherals, terminals, and databases connected by communication lines.

start-up
A young business enterprise.

stock market
A market where stocks and bonds are traded or exchanged.

vanguard
The forefront of an action or movement.

venture capitalist
A person who invests money to help businesses pursue innovative projects.

ADDITIONAL RESOURCES

SELECTED BIBLIOGRAPHY

Brandt, Richard. *One Click: Jeff Bezos and the Rise of Amazon.com.* New York: Penguin, 2011. Print.

"Jeffrey P. Bezos." *Academy of Achievement.* American Academy of Achievement, 4 May 2001. Web. 7 Dec. 2011.

Leibovich, Mark. *The New Imperialists: How Five Restless Kids Grew up to Virtually Rule Your World.* Paramus, NJ: Prentice Hall Press, 2002. Print.

Quittner, Joshua. "An Eye On The Future." *Time.* Time Inc., 27 Dec. 1999. Web. 7 Dec. 2011.

Spector, Robert. *Amazon.com: Get Big Fast.* New York: HarperBusiness, 2000. Print.

FURTHER READINGS

Robinson, Tom. *Jeff Bezos: Amazon.com Architect.* Minneapolis: Abdo, 2009. Print.

Sherman, Josepha. *Jeff Bezos: King of Amazon.* Minneapolis: Millbrook, 2001. Print.

WEB LINKS

To learn more about Amazon.com, visit ABDO Publishing Company online at **www.abdopublishing.com**. Web sites about Amazon.com are featured on our Book Links page. These links are routinely monitored and updated to provide the most current information available.

PLACES TO VISIT

Center for the History of Print Culture in Modern America
University of Wisconsin–Madison
600 North Park Street, Madison, WI 53706
608-263-2900
http://www.slis.wisc.edu/chpchome.htm
The center studies how the printed word has influenced US society.

Computer History Museum
1401 North Shoreline Boulevard, Mountain View, CA 94043
650-810-1010
http://www.computerhistory.org
The Computer History Museum holds a variety of artifacts relating to the history of computer technology. The museum's exhibits include vintage computers to the earliest calculators.

The Tech Museum of Innovation
201 South Market Street, San Jose, CA 95113
408–294–TECH (8324)
http://www.thetech.org/
This museum allows visitors to explore and experience cutting-edge technologies.

SOURCE NOTES

CHAPTER 1. A NEW WAY TO READ

1. Steven Levy. "The Future of Reading." *The Daily Beast.* Newsweek/ The Daily Beast Company, 17 Nov. 2007. Web. 2 Jan. 2012.

2. Richard Brandt. *One Click: Jeff Bezos and the Rise of Amazon.com.* New York: Penguin, 2011. Print. 135.

3. Ibid. 136.

4. Ibid. 135.

5. Karl Weber and Adrian Slywotzky. *Demand: Creating What People Love Before They Know They Want It.* New York: Random House Digital, 2011. *Google Book Search.* Web. 15 Apr. 2012.

6. "Making Digital Books into Page Turners." *Bloomberg.* Bloomberg Businessweek, 3 Sept. 2007. Web. 19 Feb. 2012.

7. Stephen Levy. "The Future of Reading." *The Daily Beast.* Newsweek/ The Daily Beast Company, 17 Nov. 2007. Web. 2 Jan. 2012.

8. Richard Brandt. *One Click: Jeff Bezos and the Rise of Amazon.com.* New York: Penguin, 2011. Print. 142.

CHAPTER 2. THE YOUNG ENTREPRENEUR

1. Richard Brandt. *One Click: Jeff Bezos and the Rise of Amazon.com.* New York: Penguin, 2011. Print. 20.

2. Ibid. 21.

3. "Jeffrey Bezos Interview." *Academy of Achievement.* American Academy of Achievement, 4 May 2001. Web. 7 Dec. 2011.

4. Robert Spector. *Amazon.com: Get Big Fast.* New York: HarperBusiness, 2000. Print. 11.

5. Richard Brandt. *One Click: Jeff Bezos and the Rise of Amazon.com.* New York: Penguin, 2011. Print. 36.

6. Ibid. 38–39.

CHAPTER 3. THE START-UP

1. Robert Spector. *Amazon.com: Get Big Fast.* New York: HarperBusiness, 2000. Print. 33.

2. Richard Brandt. *One Click: Jeff Bezos and the Rise of Amazon.com.* New York: Penguin, 2011. Print. 40.

3. Robert Spector. *Amazon.com: Get Big Fast.* New York: HarperBusiness, 2000. Print. 27.

4. "Jeffrey Bezos Interview." *Academy of Achievement.* American Academy of Achievement, 4 May 2001. Web. 7 Dec. 2011.

5. Bill Gates. "The 2009 TIME 100." *Time.* Time, 30 Apr. 2009. Web. 6 Dec. 2011.

6. Joshua Quittner. "An Eye On The Future." *Time.* Time, 27 Dec. 1999. Web. 7 Dec. 2011.

7. Robert Spector. *Amazon.com: Get Big Fast.* New York: HarperBusiness, 2000. Print. 42.

8. Joshua Cooper Ramo. "The Fast-Moving Internet Economy Has A Jungle Of Competitors . . . And Here's The King." *Time.* 27 Dec. 1999: 50. *MasterFILE Premier.* Web. 7 Dec. 2011.

9. Joshua Quittner. "An Eye On The Future." *Time.* Time, 27 Dec. 1999. Web. 7 Dec. 2011.

CHAPTER 4. EARLY SUCCESS

1. Joshua Quittner. "An Eye On The Future." *Time.* Time, 27 Dec. 1999. Web. 7 Dec. 2011.

2. Robert Spector. *Amazon.com: Get Big Fast.* New York: HarperBusiness, 2000. Print. 70–71.

3. Ibid. 74.

4. Ibid. 67.

5. Richard Brandt. *One Click: Jeff Bezos and the Rise of Amazon.com.* New York: Penguin, 2011. Print. 75.

6. Robert Spector. *Amazon.com: Get Big Fast.* New York: HarperBusiness, 2000. Print. 57.

7. Ibid. Print. 62.

8. Mark Leibovich. *The New Imperialists: How Five Restless Kids Grew up to Virtually Rule Your World.* Paramus, NJ: Prentice Hall Press, 2002. Print. 91.

9. Ibid. 89.

10. Richard Brandt. *One Click: Jeff Bezos and the Rise of Amazon.com.* New York: Penguin, 2011. Print. 70.

SOURCE NOTES CONTINUED

CHAPTER 5. STAYING AHEAD

1. Richard Brandt. *One Click: Jeff Bezos and the Rise of Amazon.com.* New York: Penguin, 2011. Print. 95.

2. Ibid. 98.

3. "Jeffrey Bezos Interview." *Academy of Achievement.* American Academy of Achievement, 4 May 2001. Web. 12 Dec. 2011.

4. William C. Taylor. "Who's Writing the Book on Web Business?" *Fast Company.* Fast Company, 31 Oct. 1996. Web. 7 Dec. 2011.

5. Richard Brandt. *One Click: Jeff Bezos and the Rise of Amazon.com.* New York: Penguin, 2011. Print. 96.

CHAPTER 6. DIVERSIFYING AND EXPANDING

1. Richard Brandt. *One Click: Jeff Bezos and the Rise of Amazon.com.* New York: Penguin, 2011. Print. 111.

2. Ibid. 112.

3. Robert Spector. *Amazon.com: Get Big Fast.* New York: HarperBusiness, 2000. Print. 148.

4. Richard Brandt. *One Click: Jeff Bezos and the Rise of Amazon.com.* New York: Penguin, 2011. Print. 107.

CHAPTER 7. RIDING HIGH

1. Joshua Quittner. "An Eye On The Future." *Time.* Time, 27 Dec. 1999. Web. 7 Dec. 2011.

2. Robert Spector. *Amazon.com: Get Big Fast.* New York: HarperBusiness, 2000. Print. 216.

3. Richard Brandt. *One Click: Jeff Bezos and the Rise of Amazon.com.* New York: Penguin, 2011. Print. 121.

4. Robert Spector. *Amazon.com: Get Big Fast.* New York: HarperBusiness, 2000. Print. 201.

5. Joshua Quittner. "An Eye On The Future." *Time.* Time, 27 Dec. 1999. Web. 7 Dec. 2011.

6. Robert Spector. *Amazon.com: Get Big Fast.* New York: HarperBusiness, 2000. Print. 234.

CHAPTER 8. SURVIVING AND THRIVING

1. Richard Brandt. *One Click: Jeff Bezos and the Rise of Amazon.com.* New York: Penguin, 2011. Print. 128.

2. Ibid. 129.

3. Mark Leibovich. *The New Imperialists: How Five Restless Kids Grew up to Virtually Rule Your World.* Paramus, NJ: Prentice Hall Press, 2002. Print. 96.

4. "Jeff Bezos Biography." *Academy of Achievement.* American Academy of Achievement, 9 Aug. 2010. Web. 7 Dec. 2011.

CHAPTER 9. AMAZON TODAY

1. Steven Levy. "Jeff Bezos Owns the Web in More Ways Than You Think." *Wired.* Condé Nast, 13 Nov. 2011. Web. 10 Mar. 2012.

2. Richard Brandt. *One Click: Jeff Bezos and the Rise of Amazon.com.* New York: Penguin, 2011. Print. 152.

3. Ibid. 151–152.

4. Ibid. 157.

5. Bob Minzesheimer. "Is There Hope for Small Bookstores in a Digital Age?" *USA Today.* Gannett, 10 Nov. 2011. Web. 10 Mar. 2012.

6. Theodore F. di Stefano. "Traditional Publishers: Refresh Your Business or Fade to Irrelevance." *Ecommerce Times.* ECT News Network, 5 Jan. 2012. Web. 6 Jan. 2012.

7. "Supporting the Writing Community." *Amazon.com.* Amazon.com Inc., n.d. Web. 5 Jan. 2012.

8. Richard Brandt. *One Click: Jeff Bezos and the Rise of Amazon.com.* New York: Penguin, 2011. Print. 17.

9. Husna Haq. "5 Discoveries Made about the Amazon Kindle Tablet." *Christian Science Monitor,* 27 Sept. 2011. *MasterFILE Premier.* Web. 9 Jan. 2012.

10. Joshua Cooper Ramo. "The Fast-Moving Internet Economy Has A Jungle Of Competitors . . . And Here's The King." *Time,* 27 Dec. 1999: 50. *MasterFILE Premier.* Web. 9 Jan. 2012.

11. Richard Brandt. *One Click: Jeff Bezos and the Rise of Amazon.com.* New York: Penguin, 2011. Print. 191.

INDEX

ABOUT THE AUTHOR

Erika Wittekind is a freelance writer and editor living in Wisconsin. She has a bachelor of arts degree in journalism and political science from Bradley University. Wittekind has covered education and government for several community newspapers, winning an award for best local news story from the Minnesota Newspapers Association for 2002. She has been working in children's nonfiction since 2008.

PHOTO CREDITS

Ted S. Warren/AP Images, cover, 38, 97 (top); Mark Lennihan/AP Images, 6, 17, 98, 99 (bottom); Bebeto Matthews/AP Images, 11; Seth Poppel/Yearbook Library, 18; Denise Bush/iStockphoto, 23; Kimberly White/Bloomberg/Getty Images, 27; Tom Bible/Alamy, 28; Katherine Welles/Shutterstock Images, 34; Andy Rogers/AP Images, 37; Michael Grecco/Getty Images, 40; Dino Vournas/Reuters, 47; Barry Sweet/AP Images, 48, 54, 78, 96; John Zich/Chicago Board Options Exchange/AP Images, 57; Paul Souders/Getty Images, 58; Cyberstock/Alamy, 61, 97 (bottom); Adrian Sherratt/Alamy, 65; Reuters, 66, 99 (top); Richard Drew/AP Images, 69; Andrea Zanchi/iStockphoto, 75; Robert Spencer/AP Images, 76; Kathy Willens/AP Images, 82; Web Pix/Alamy, 85; Matthew Staver/Bloomberg/Getty Images, 86; Andrew Harrer/Bloomberg/Getty Images, 88; Bloomberg/Getty Images, 95

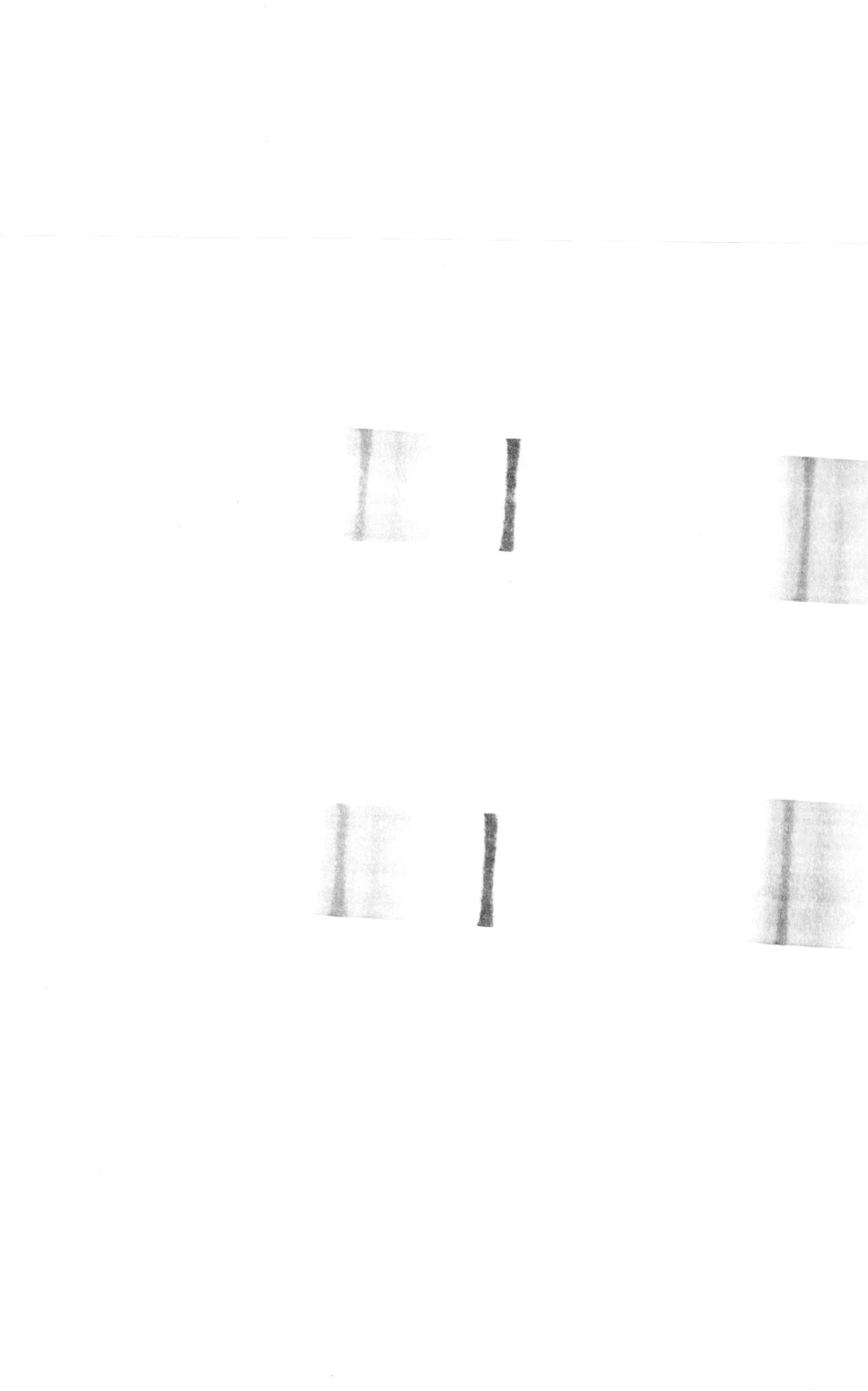